A LOOK AT PRIMARY SOURCES

POEMS

BY KRISTEN RAJCZAK NELSON

Gareth Stevens PUBLISHING

CRASHCOURSE

Please visit our website, www.garethstevens.com. For a free color catalog of all our high-quality books, call toll free 1-800-542-2595 or fax 1-877-542-2596.

Cataloging-in-Publication Data

Names: Nelson, Kristen Rajczak.
Title: Poems / Kristen Rajczak Nelson.
Description: New York : Gareth Stevens, 2024. | Series: A look at primary sources | Includes glossary, index, and bibliographic information
Identifiers: ISBN 9781538287583 (pbk) | ISBN 9781538287590 (library bound) | ISBN 9781538287606 (ebook)
Subjects: LCSH: Information resources-- Juvenile literature | Poetry-- Juvenile literature
Classification: LCC PN688 N45 2024 | DDC 800--dc24

First Edition

Published in 2024 by
Gareth Stevens Publishing
2544 Clinton Street
Buffalo, NY 14224

Designer: Claire Wrazin
Editor: Kristen Rajczak Nelson

Photo credits: Cover (poem), pp. 5 (newspaper and poems), 9, 19, 23, 25 (newspaper clipping) Courtesy of Library of Congress; series art (background texture) Verbena/Shutterstock.com; series art (cover typeface) Gleb Guralnyk/Shutterstock.com; pp. 5 (photos), 21, 25 (background), 27 Everett Collection/Shutterstock.com; series art (photo frame) Nataliia K/Shutterstock.com; p. 7 (main) George Tolkachev/Shutterstock.com; p. 7 (sun) Zayats_art/Shutterstock.com; p. 11 Alexander Gold/Shutterstock.com; p. 13 Stephen Parker/Alamy Stock Photo; p. 15 File:Seamus_Heaney.jpg/Wikimedia Commons; p. 15 (photo frame) shyshak roman/Shutterstock.com; p. 17 Soloviova Liudmyla/Shutterstock.com; p. 27 (frame) Hintau Aliaksei/Shutterstock.com; p. 29 Natalia Lebedinskaia/Shutterstock.com.

Printed in the United States of America

CPSIA compliance information: Batch #CS24GS: For further information contact Gareth Stevens at 1-800-542-2595.

CONTENTS

Words in the glossary appear in **bold** type the first time they are used in the text.

UNDERSTAND FIRSTHAND

Primary sources are the firsthand accounts of people who lived during a time. They may tell what someone saw or how they felt about an important event, or happening. Poems are primary sources that can teach about history, poets' lives, and writing!

MAKE THE GRADE

Other primary sources include letters, newspapers, and photographs.

WHAT IS A POEM?

A poem is a piece of writing. It may have a rhythm, or a regular pattern of sounds. It may have rhyme, or use words that have the same ending sounds. They often use flowery language to **express** feelings or **describe** a scene.

MAKE THE GRADE

Poems can be long or short. Poems called haikus are just three lines long in English!

Poems may follow a set of rules. Sonnets, for example, have 14 lines and a certain rhythm and rhyme. However, some poems follow no rules! They have no rhythm, rhyme, or form. Any poem may be used as a primary source at times.

MAKE THE GRADE

Poems may also be secondary sources. These kinds of sources comment on or **interpret** primary sources. They may look back on something that happened in history.

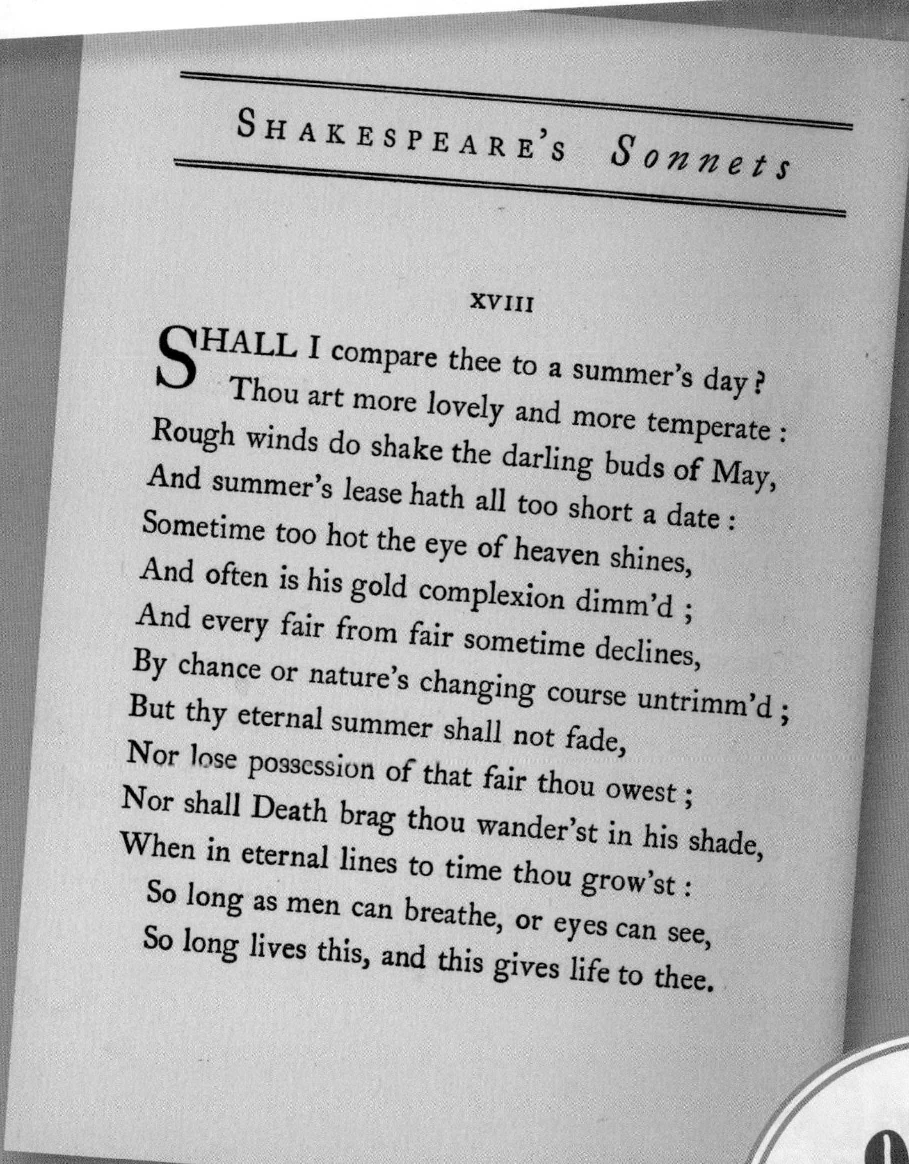

SHAKESPEARE'S *Sonnets*

XVIII

SHALL I compare thee to a summer's day?
Thou art more lovely and more temperate:
Rough winds do shake the darling buds of May,
And summer's lease hath all too short a date:
Sometime too hot the eye of heaven shines,
And often is his gold complexion dimm'd;
And every fair from fair sometime declines,
By chance or nature's changing course untrimm'd;
But thy eternal summer shall not fade,
Nor lose possession of that fair thou owest;
Nor shall Death brag thou wander'st in his shade,
When in eternal lines to time thou grow'st:
So long as men can breathe, or eyes can see,
So long lives this, and this gives life to thee.

ANY TEXT WILL DO

You don't need the original **manuscript** of a poem to use it as a primary source. Copies of poems found in books or online are still primary sources most often. What the poem says is what you are most likely studying.

MAKE THE GRADE

You would need the manuscript of a poem if you were studying the handwriting, printing, or papermaking of the time it was written!

ABOUT THE POET

Poems are used as primary sources to learn about the poet, or person who wrote the poem. Poems may be autobiographical, or telling about something that happened in the poet's life. They may express how the poet felt about changes in their life.

MAKE THE GRADE

Maya Angelou was a poet known for her autobiographical writing. Two of her most famous poems are "Still I Rise" and "On the Pulse of Morning."

It can be tricky to know if a poem is autobiographical! Even if a poet uses first-person pronouns like "I" or "me," the poem's **speaker** may be made up. Sometimes a poet will say a poem is about their life though.

MAKE THE GRADE

The poems of Northern Irish poet Seamus Heaney include a lot of autobiographical **details**. He wrote about problems in his country and losing friends.

People studying a poet interpret what the poet wrote. They use clues in the poems' themes to learn more about a poet's life. They look at what words the poet chose to use. These let the reader know how the poet felt or saw something.

MAKE THE GRADE

A poem's theme is the poet's message. It's the meaning they are trying to get across to the reader.

ON WRITING

Poems can be used as primary sources to learn about writing. By looking at a **rough draft** of a poem and comparing it to the final poem, readers see the poet at work. It shows how important **revision** is when writing.

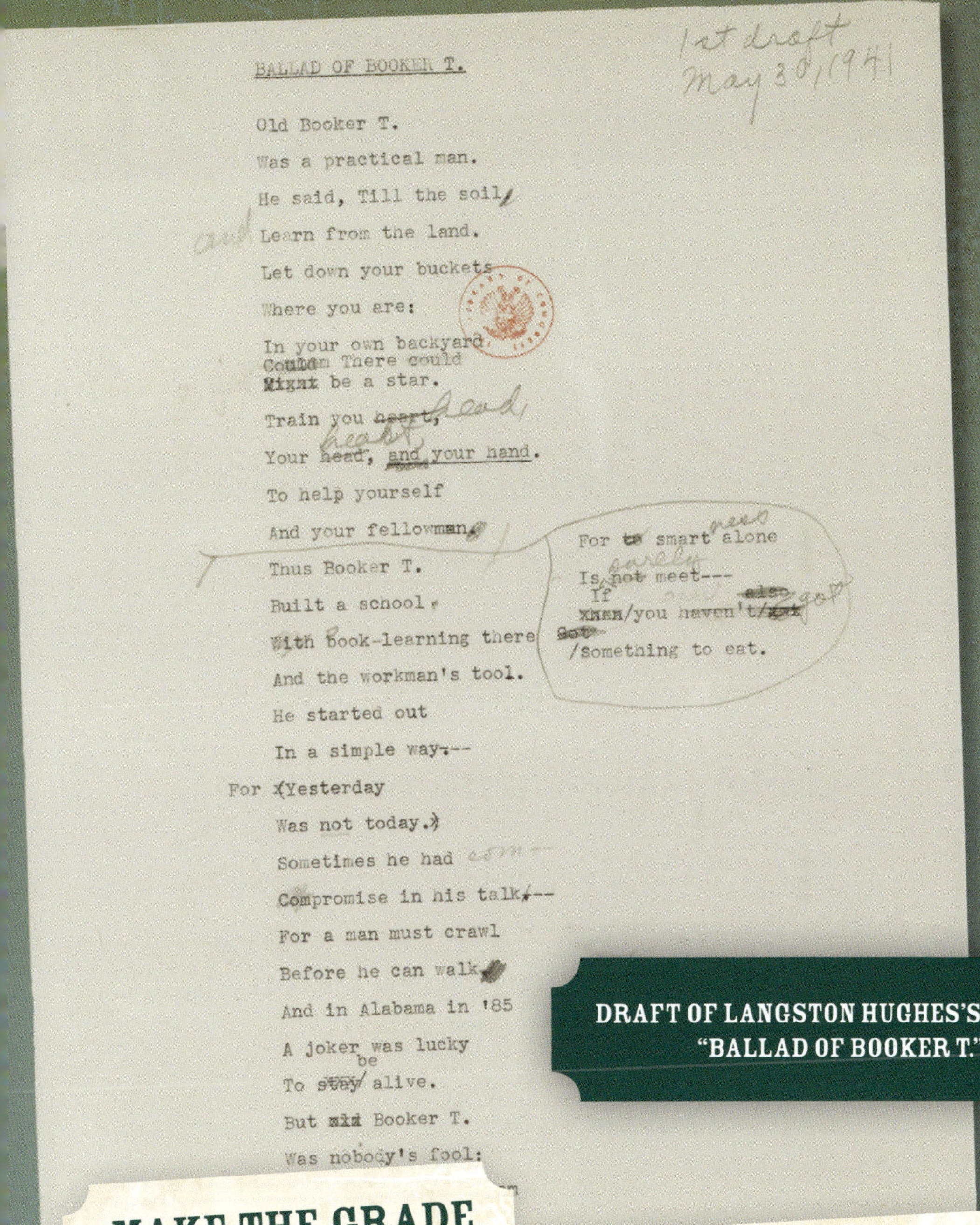

BALLAD OF BOOKER T.

1st draft
May 30, 1941

Old Booker T.
Was a practical man.
He said, Till the soil
and Learn from the land.
Let down your buckets
Where you are:
In your own backyard
There could
Be a star.
Train you head,
Your heart, and your hand.
To help yourself
And your fellowman.

For smartness alone
Is surely meet---
If you haven't got
Something to eat.

Thus Booker T.
Built a school
With book-learning there
And the workman's tool.
He started out
In a simple way---
For (Yesterday
Was not today.)
Sometimes he had
Compromise in his talk---
For a man must crawl
Before he can walk
And in Alabama in '85
A joker was lucky
To be alive.
But Booker T.
Was nobody's fool:

DRAFT OF LANGSTON HUGHES'S "BALLAD OF BOOKER T."

MAKE THE GRADE

Drafts let readers see that even the most famous poets had trouble getting their work just right sometimes!

Poet William Wordsworth wrote his first **version** of "The Prelude" around 1798. He continued working on it for many more years! **Scholars** have compared many versions to see what he changed. They learned about how he created his work.

WILLIAM WORDSWORTH

MAKE THE GRADE

"The Prelude" is also an autobiographical work. Wordsworth wrote about his life and how he felt about writing poetry.

WINDOW TO HISTORY

Like many primary sources, poems can be used to learn about a time in history. Poems have often been written about major historical events. They are studied to learn more about the time period during which they were written.

The Nation Mourns.

From all churches
Sad and slow,
Toll the bells
The knell of woe.

Hark! their sad and solemn notes attend
Abraham Lincoln to his last way's end.

Dead silence mutely hovers
Above grave's dreary strand,
With sable pall it covers
The Leader of Our Land.

Despairing men are wringing
In vain their hands here wound,
The Orphan's wail is winning
No solace from its ground.

The nightingales' caroling
Sounds never in its womb;
True Patriots tears are rolling
But on the mossy tomb.

Published by Chas. Magnus, 12 Frankfort St. N.Y.

MAKE THE GRADE

"The Nation Mourns" was written after President Abraham Lincoln was killed in 1865.

During World War I (1914–1918), many U.S. soldiers wrote poetry. Some of these poems were printed in newspapers. The poems expressed how the soldiers felt about the war, being so far from home, and even the fun of living in camps together.

MAKE THE GRADE

Poems show the feelings and ideas of everyday people in history. That's because anyone can write a poem if they want to!

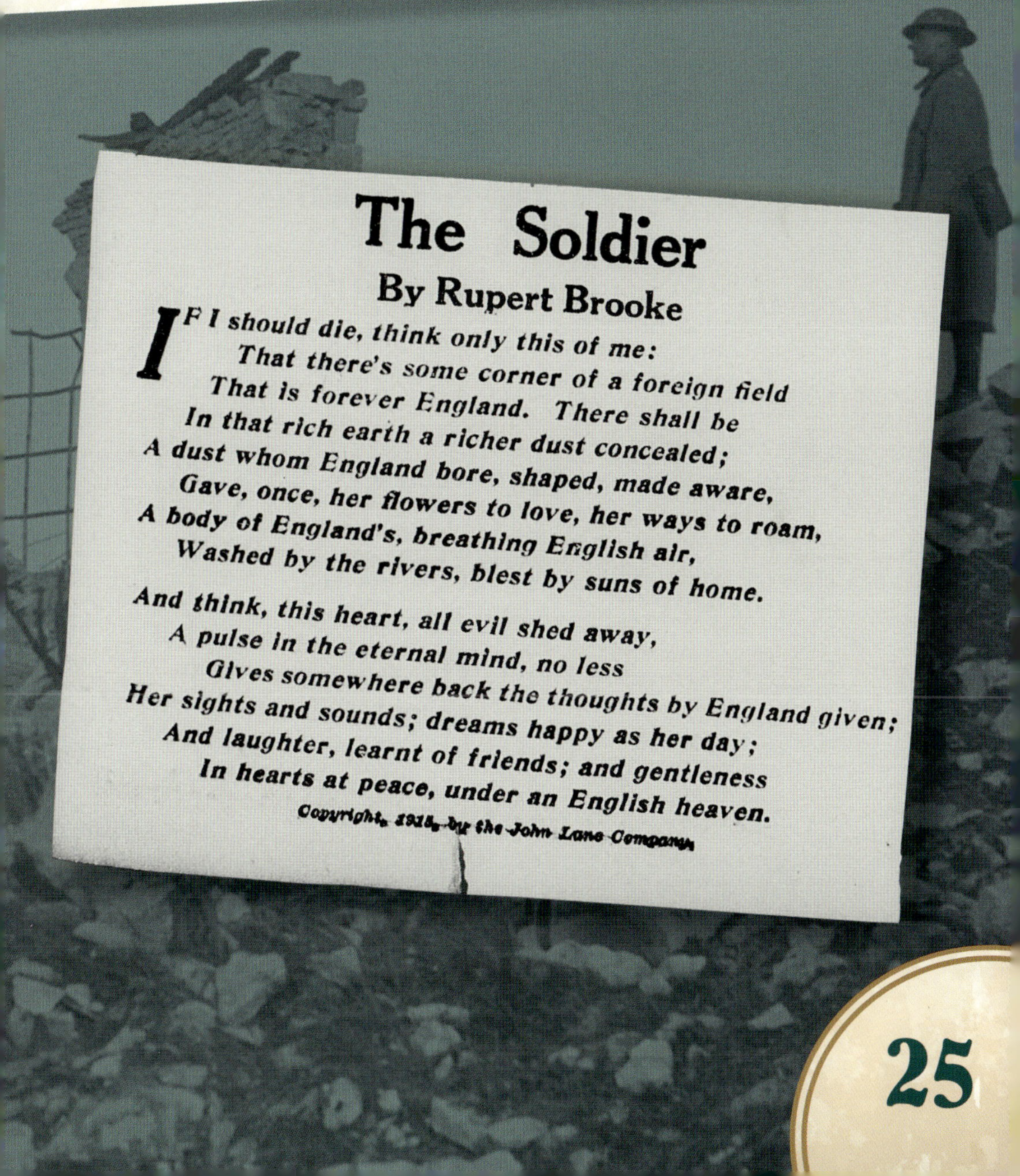

The Soldier

By Rupert Brooke

IF I should die, think only this of me:
That there's some corner of a foreign field
That is forever England. There shall be
In that rich earth a richer dust concealed;
A dust whom England bore, shaped, made aware,
Gave, once, her flowers to love, her ways to roam,
A body of England's, breathing English air,
Washed by the rivers, blest by suns of home.

And think, this heart, all evil shed away,
A pulse in the eternal mind, no less
Gives somewhere back the thoughts by England given;
Her sights and sounds; dreams happy as her day;
And laughter, learnt of friends; and gentleness
In hearts at peace, under an English heaven.

Copyright, 1915, by the John Lane Company

FURTHER THE CAUSE

Poetry has often been a place for writers to express their beliefs about a cause. For example, many poets wrote about the civil rights movement of the 1960s. These are good primary sources to learn what a person or group thought.

MAKE THE GRADE

Poems that look back at a cause or event—but were not written at the time of the cause or event—would be considered secondary sources.

DISCOVER POETRY!

Poetry today is just as often written online as in a book! You can find the work of poets old and new at your local library. Blogs, websites, and social media sites are modern platforms for poetry. These can all be used as primary sources!

MAKE THE GRADE

Do you write poetry? Someday, it may be used as a primary source to learn about you or the time you lived in!

USING A POEM AS A PRIMARY SOURCE

Visit your local library or the Children's Poetry Archive website (*childrens.poetryarchive.org*) to find a poem. You will use it as a primary source to learn about the poet and the time when it was written.

Read the poem. *What do you think it's about?*

Find out who wrote the poem. Then, read it again.

- *Does anything in the poem tell you about the poet? How do you know?*
- *What is the theme or message of the poem? Why do you think the poet is trying to tell the reader this?*

Find out more about the poet. *Does anything in the poem support what you learn?*

Look up when the poem was written. Find out what happened in history around then.

Read the poem with the time period in mind. *Does the poem tell the reader anything about the time period? How do you know?*

GLOSSARY

describe: To tell what something looks, smells, or sounds like.

detail: A small part of something.

express: To make known.

interpret: To explain the meaning of something.

manuscript: The original copy of a piece of writing before it is printed.

revision: A change that improves a piece of writing.

rough draft: The first version of a piece of writing that needs to be edited and rewritten in places.

scholar: Someone who has a great deal of knowledge about a subject.

speaker: The voice, or narrator, of a poem.

version: A form of something that is different from others.

FOR MORE INFORMATION

BOOKS

Dickinson, Emily. Ryan G. Van Cleave, ed. *The Illustrated Emily Dickinson.* Fresno, CA: Bushel & Peck Books, 2022.

Watson, Renée. *Maya's Song*. New York, NY: Harper, an imprint of Harper Collins Publishers, 2022.

WEBSITE

Children's Poetry Archive
childrens.poetryarchive.org/
Find your new favorite poem and listen to it here.

Publisher's note to educators and parents: Our editors have carefully reviewed these websites to ensure that they are suitable for students. Many websites change frequently, however, and we cannot guarantee that a site's future contents will continue to meet our high standards of quality and educational value. Be advised that students should be closely supervised whenever they access the internet.

INDEX